EARTH'S smallest SUPERHEROES

MICROBES

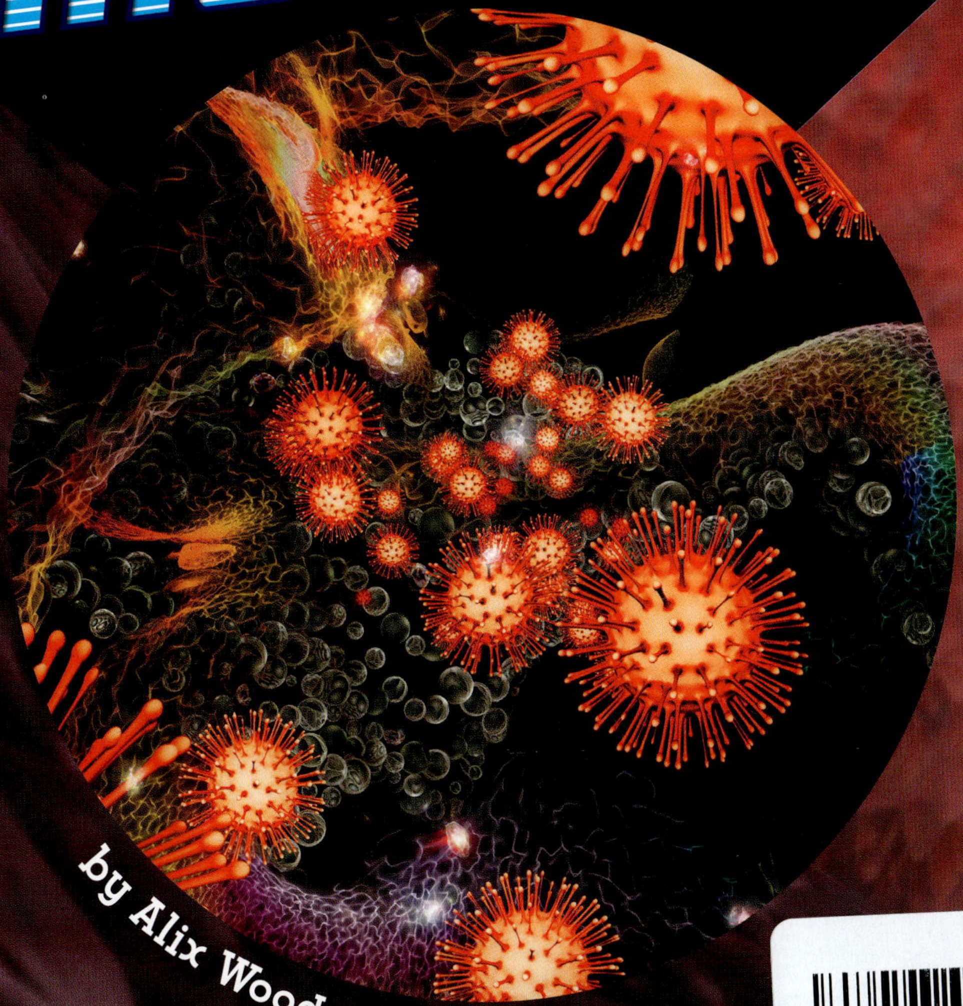

by Alix Wood

With thanks to:
Professor Abigail McQuatters-Gollop
Professor of Marine Conservation
School of Biological and Marine Science,
University of Plymouth, Plymouth, Devon, UK

Ruby Tuesday Books

Published in 2026 by Ruby Tuesday Books Ltd.

Editors: Ruth Owen & Mark J. Sachner
Design & Production: Alix Wood

Picture credits:
Alamy: 26C (Operation 2021); Public Domain: 17T; Ruby Tuesday Books: 11B, 25B, 26B, 28T; Science Photo Library: 7T (Steve Gschmeissner), 7B (Frank Fox), 8T (Henning Dalhoff), 9T (Martin Oeggerli), 10TR (Eye of Science), 15T (Eye of Science), 15C (Ray Simons), 16B (Eye of Science), 20TL (Steve Gschmeissner), 27B (Volker Steger); Shutterstock: Cover (Marko Aliaksandr/dahool23), 1 (agsandrew), 3 (Helga_KOV/Darinov Art), 4 (studiovin/Tartila/studiovin), 5T (Max Zafiro), 5C (Lightspring), 6B (Connect Images-Curated), 8C (Kletr), 10TL (Harry Powell), 10B (Lightspring), 11T (Gallwis), 12B (Kateryna Kon), 13T (Design_Cells), 13B (Designua), 14T (Sardo Michael), 14BL (Kateryna Kon), 14BR (Gulf MG), 16T (Joerg Beuge), 16C (DronG), 17C (Kateryna Kon), 17B (Fahroni), 18T (CI Photos), 18B (PeopleImages.com Yuri A/Sensvector/Kateryna Kon/Vitalij Terescsuk), 19T (Prostock-studio), 19B (Marilyn Barbone), 20TR (Lyubov Levitskaya), 20BL (Love Employee), 21L (SK Chavan), 22T (gresei), 22C (Yeti Studio), 22BL (mineral vision), 22BR (barmalini), 23TR (Imageman), 23T (kwanchai.c), 23C (tristan tan), 23B (Kaiskynet Studio), 24T (ixpert), 24B (Rido), 25TL (Clara Bastian), 25TR (Fran Marin), 27T (Limbitech/Kateryna Kon), 28B (J_R Images), 29T (William Edge), 29C (Sarawut Chainawarat), 29B (Red Confidential); Superstock: 6T (Steve Gschmeissner), 12T (Everett Collection), 21R (Steve Gschmeissner), 24C (Choksawatdikorn/SPL); Alix Wood: 9B, 15B.

Library of Congress Control Number: 2025936402

Print (Hardback) ISBN 978-1-78856-459-5
Print (Paperback) ISBN 978-1-78856-460-1
ePub ISBN 978-1-78856-461-8

Published in Minneapolis, MN
Printed in the United States

www.rubytuesdaybooks.com

Contents

Tiny but Mighty

This is a book about things SO small they can only be seen with powerful microscopes.

In fact, they are so tiny, a billion of them could fit on this period.

What? I thought this was a book about superheroes.

These microscopic living things are microbes.

Microbes are found everywhere. They live in air, in water, in soil, in scorching deserts, and in freezing Antarctica.

There are some types of microbes that may actually NOT be alive. But more on that later!

Microbes are found in candy bars, yogurt, even in your grilled cheese sandwich.

You can't see them, but about 38 trillion microbes are on and inside YOUR body—right at this moment!

Ugh. That's weird, but also kind of incredible. So why are they superheroes?

Microbes are essential to our world. Without them, our bodies could not digest food or fight off diseases.

Some microbes make the oxygen we breathe. Others fight pollution. And these tiny superheroes help make medicines that save millions of lives every year!

Wow! That's pretty impressive. Please tell me more.

Let's Meet Some Microbes

Microbes are divided into five main groups. And in every group, there are superheroes and super-villains.

Bacteria

Most bacteria are super helpful. But some bacteria can make us sick.

All living things are made up of tiny parts called cells. A human is made of 30 trillion cells. A bacterium is made of just one cell.

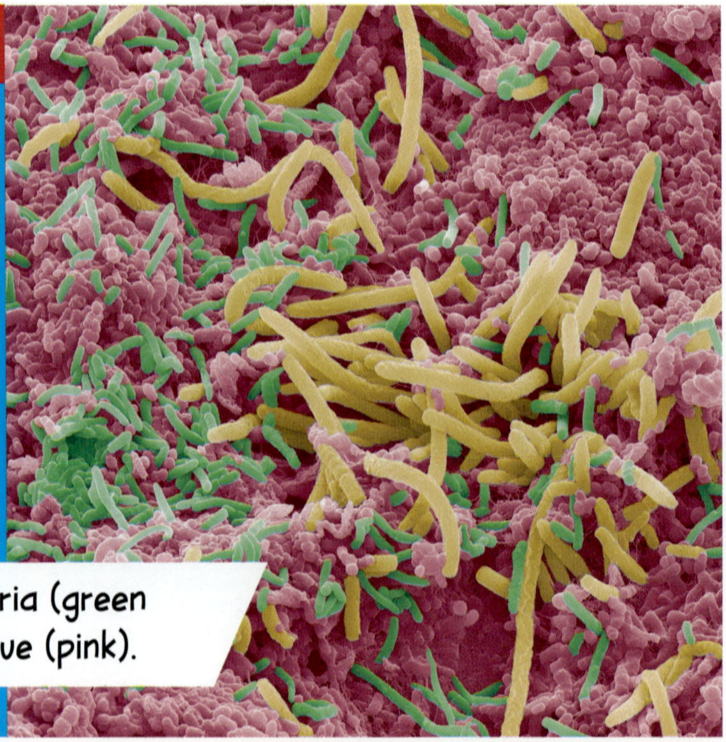

A close-up SEM image of bacteria (green and yellow) on a person's tongue (pink).

Archaea

These single-celled microbes are a lot like bacteria, but they don't cause diseases.

Scientists used to think archaea were bacteria. However, in the 1970s they were classified as their own group. A single one of these archaea is called an archaeon.

Scanning Electron Microscopes (SEMs) allow scientists to look at super-small things. The microscope is connected to a computer that creates an on-screen SEM image of the item the scientist is studying.

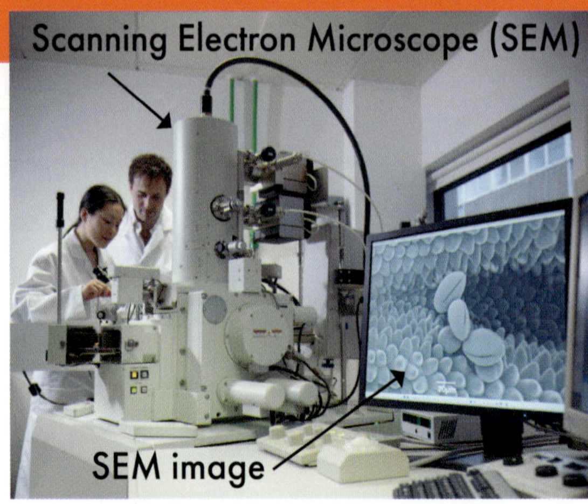

Viruses

Viruses are the smallest of all the microbes. They can only survive inside the cells of other living things. Viruses cause illnesses such as colds and flu.

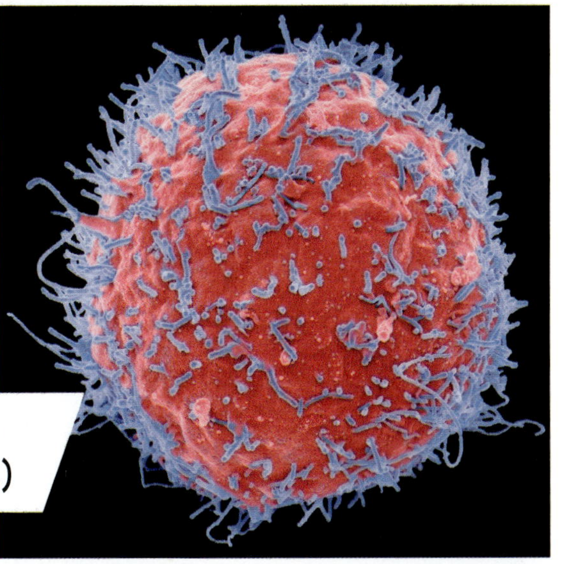

An SEM image of a human body cell infected with flu virus (blue strands)

Protists

Protists are single-celled living things. They are not animals, plants, or fungi, but they sometimes look and act a lot like these bigger living things.

An SEM image of plant-like protists that live in ponds

Fungi

Mushrooms, toadstools, and molds are all fungi. We can see mushrooms, but some types of fungi are so small, they are thought of as microbes.

So what are germs? Are they a type of microbe?

Good question! We usually describe microbes that make us sick as "germs." So any bacteria, virus, fungus, or protist that causes illness can be called a germ.

Earth's Oldest Microbes

Bacteria are one of the earliest known life forms. They have been around for at least 3.5 billion years.

Ancient bacteria called cyanobacteria lived in Earth's prehistoric oceans. They began to make oxygen and helped create a world where other living things could survive.

Cyanobacteria

Scientists estimate there are about 8.7 million different species, or types, of living things on Earth. More than three-quarters are species of bacteria!

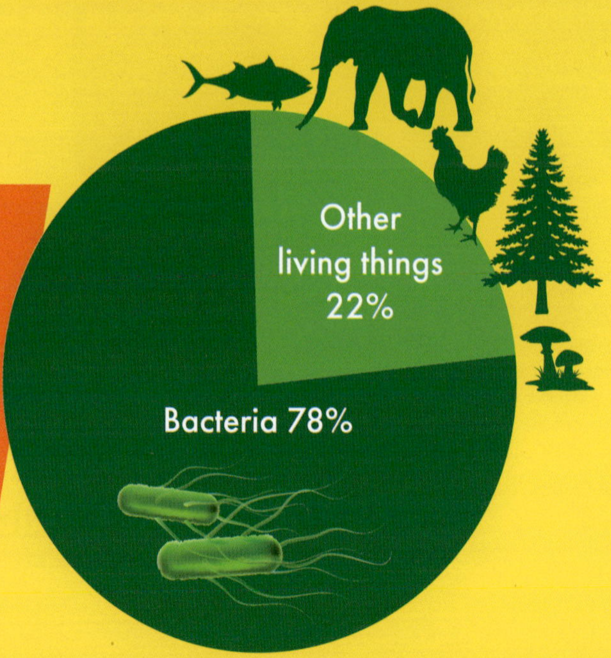

Super-Sticky Bacteria

There's a type of bacteria that produces a super-sticky glue—eight times stronger than super glue! These microbes live in lakes and rivers and stick to boats and underwater pipes.

Scientists think their waterproof glue could be used in wet places to repair ships or seal up water pipes. It could even be used by doctors to close up wounds.

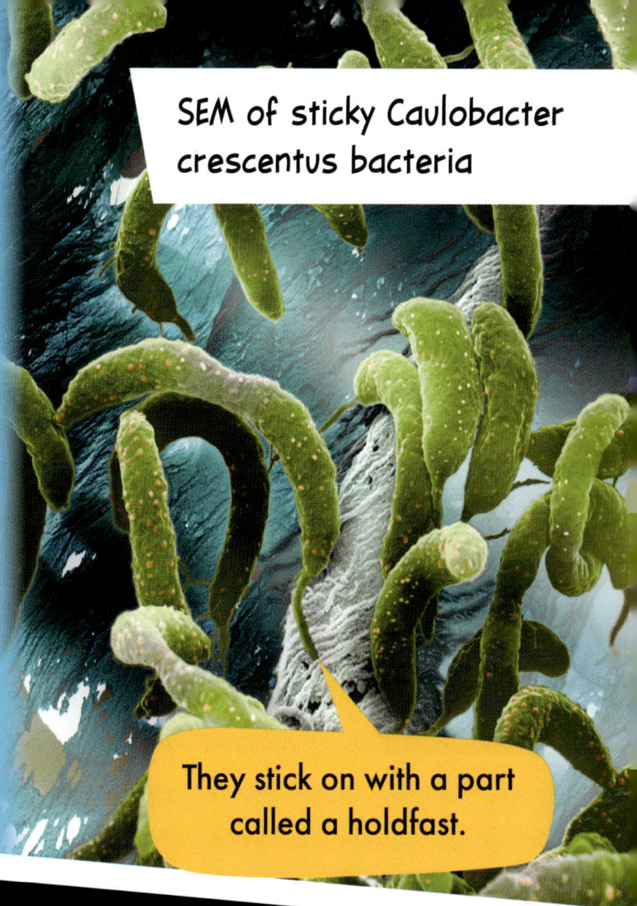

SEM of sticky *Caulobacter crescentus* bacteria

Magnetic Microbes

Microbes known as magnetotactic bacteria contain tiny magnetic parts called magnetosomes.

Scientists are studying these bacteria to see if they could carry medicines directly to a place inside a sick person. Doctors would use magnets to move and guide the magnetic bacteria on the outside of the patient's body.

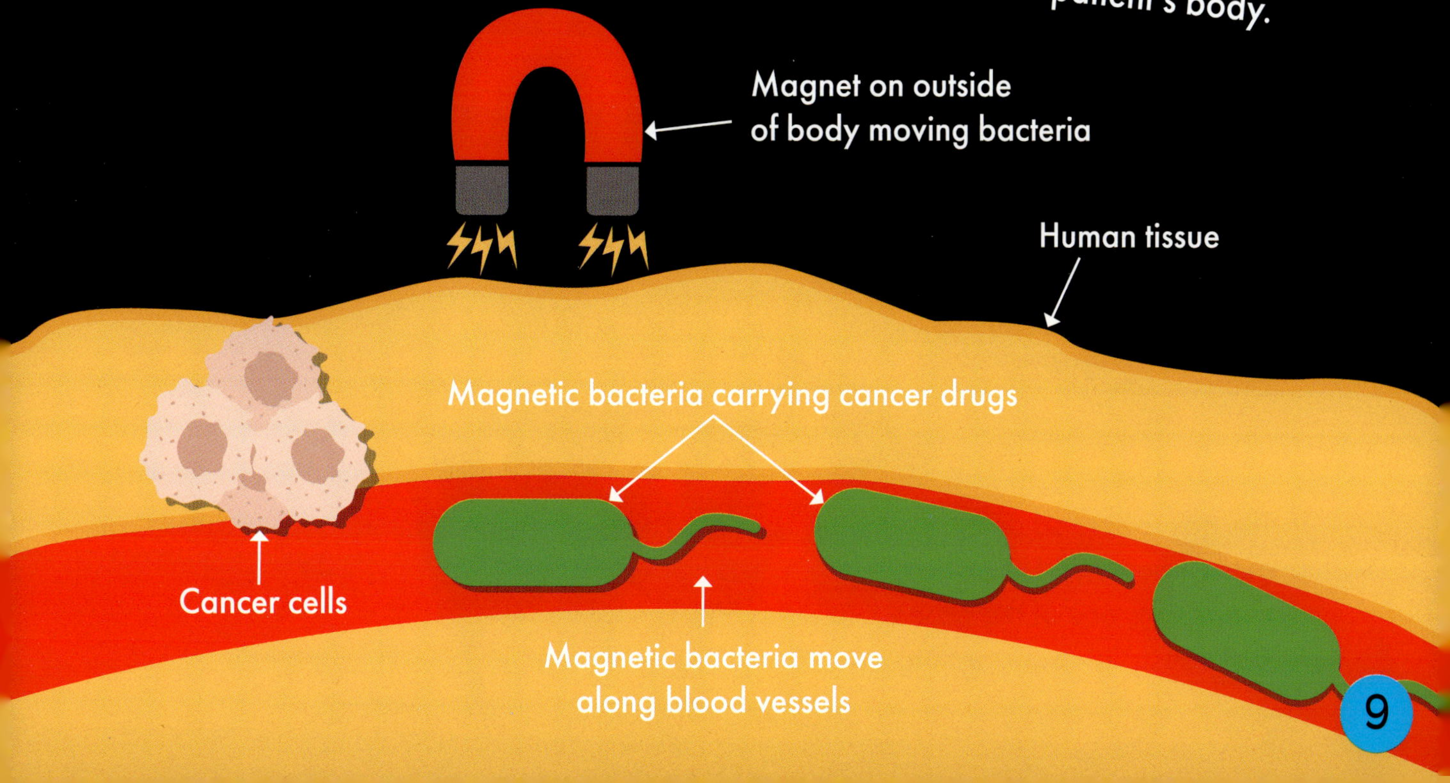

The Extremophiles

Archaea are the true tough guys of the microbial world. They've been found living in oil wells, inside rock, and in solid ice.

Archaea have an extra-tough, outer cell wall that helps protect them in harsh environments.

Archaea even live in hot springs. The near-boiling, acidic water in a hot spring would instantly kill most other living things!

A hot spring at Yellowstone National Park

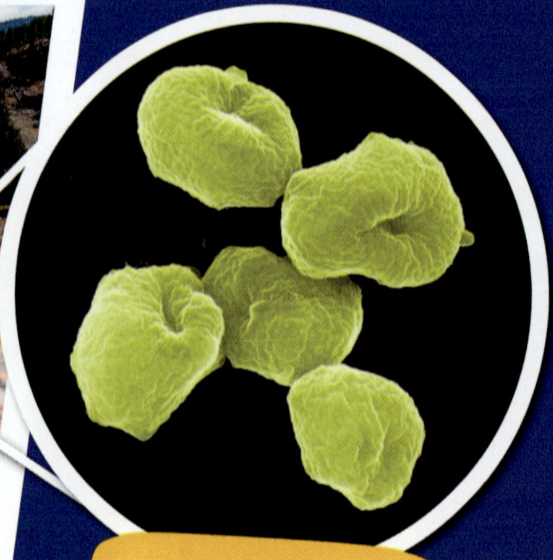

An archaeon called Sulfolobus

Some archaea live in cows' stomachs. They help break down grass and other food. As they do this, the microbes produce methane gas.

The gas is burped and farted out by the cows. Unfortunately, methane is one of the gases that causes global warming.

Archaea have also been found in the super-hot liquids of hydrothermal vents, deep under the ocean.

An archaeon called Strain 121 was discovered in a hydrothermal vent. It can survive temperatures of 250°F (121°C)—hotter than boiling point. This is the temperature hospital sterilizing machines reach to kill germs on surgical instruments.

Scientists call archaea extremophiles, which means, "extreme-loving."

An archaeon called Nanoarchaeum is one of the smallest living things ever discovered. It's just 400 nanometers wide.

How small is a nanometer?

It's seriously small. For example, a human hair is about 80,000 nanometers wide!

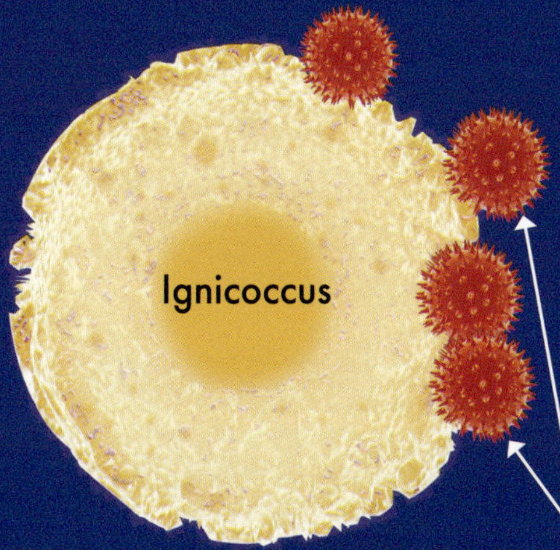

Nanoarchaeum is a parasite. It lives and feeds on a bigger archaeon, called Ignicoccus.

Viruses: Good Guys or Bad Guys?

When I hear the word "virus," I think bad guy!

You're right. Viruses are the smallest, simplest microbe. But they can be deadly.

Influenza, or flu, is a super-villain virus. A worldwide outbreak of flu during 1918 to 1920 killed around 50 million people!

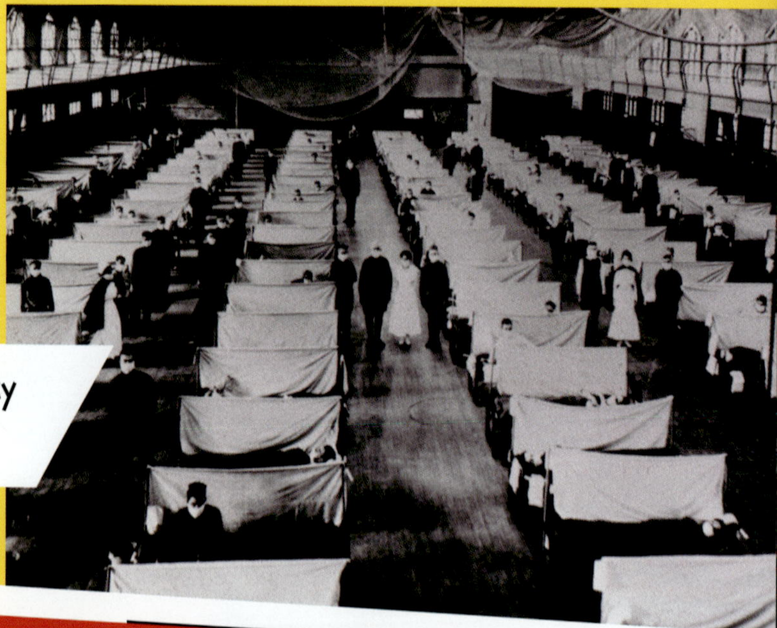

A school gym turned into an emergency hospital for flu patients in 1918.

Covid-19 is another serious disease. It is caused by a virus named SARS-CoV-2. In 2020, this virus spread around the world, causing a pandemic.

SARS-CoV-2 virus infecting a person's lungs

Viruses cannot survive on their own. They have to live in the cells of living things such as humans, animals, or bacteria. Because of this, some scientists think viruses are not actually living things themselves. Other scientists disagree and think they are alive.

So are viruses always the bad guys?

No! Some viruses are helpful. Bacteriophages, or phages for short, are superhero viruses that kill bacteria.

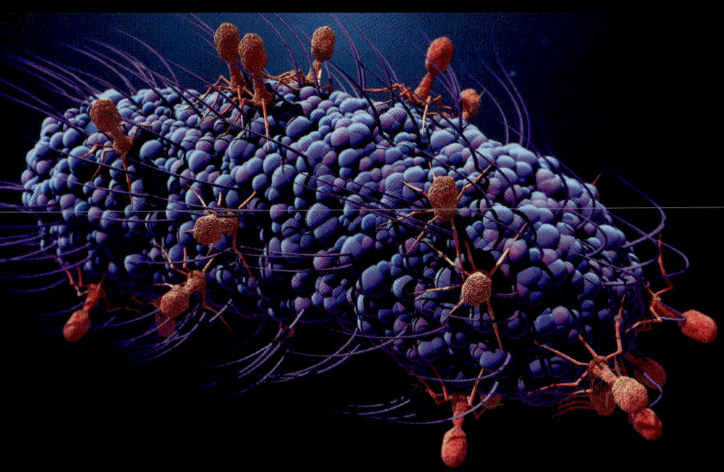

An illustration of phages attacking a bacterium

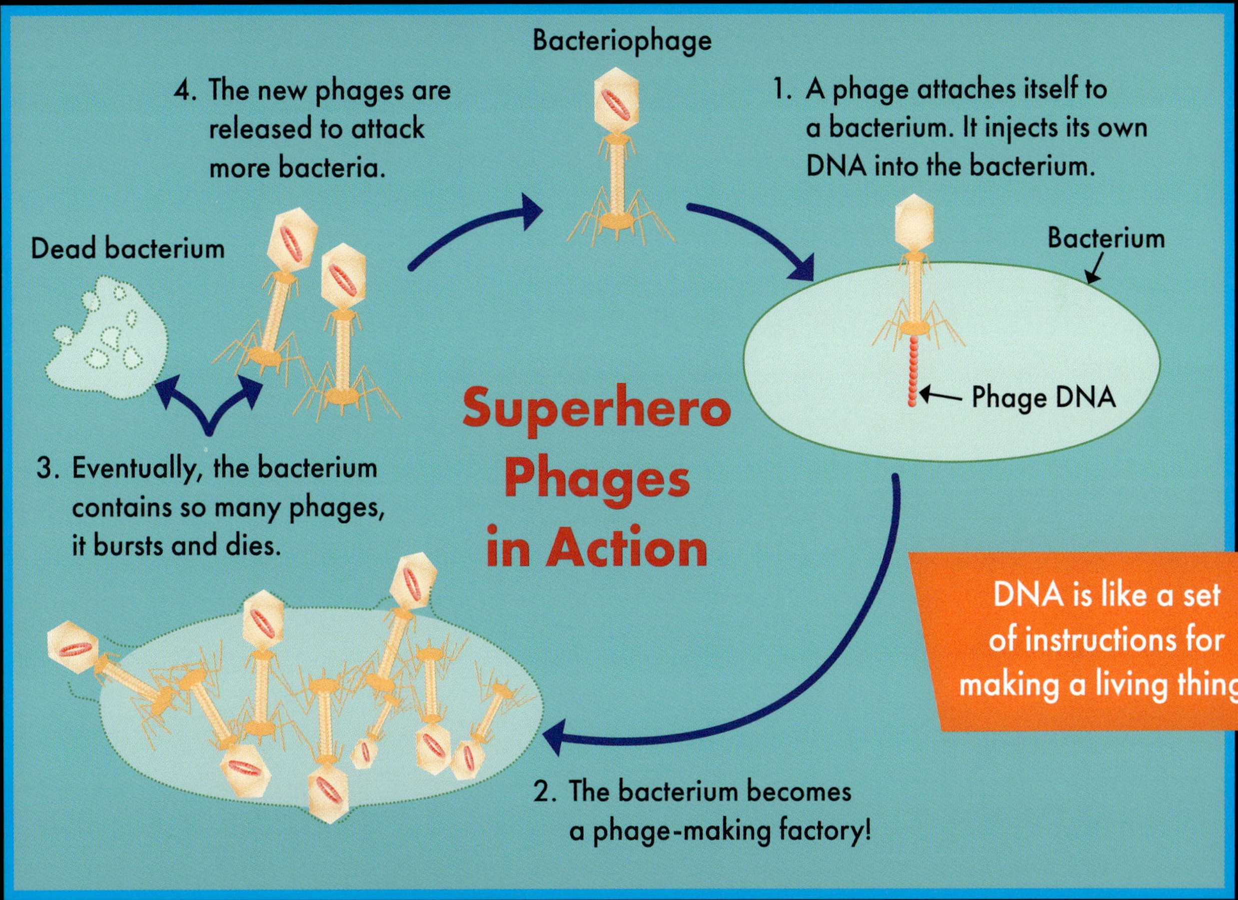

DNA is like a set of instructions for making a living thing.

So how big is a phage?

If a phage were the size of this comma, a person would be about 4 miles (6.5 km) tall.

Wow! That IS tiny!

Doctors hope that phages can be used in patients' bodies to kill off bacteria that cause illnesses.

Let's Meet Some Protists

So tell me again. What exactly are protists?

This group includes a mixture of different microscopic living things—from deadly parasites to living slimes that can solve puzzles!

Algae are tiny, plant-like protists that live in water. They sometimes team up to form large, floating strings or mats.

Strings made of single-celled algae

Plasmodium is a protist that causes the disease malaria. A mosquito bites a person to feed on their blood. If the mosquito is infected with Plasmodium, it injects this parasite into the person's body.

The Plasmodium infects the person's blood and makes them seriously ill.

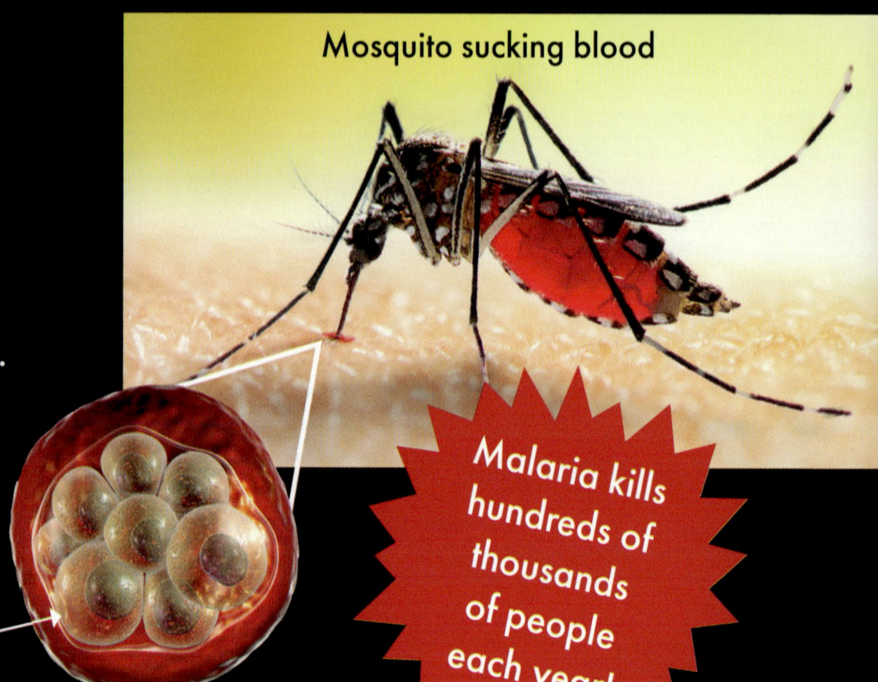

Mosquito sucking blood

Plasmodium

Infected human red blood cell

Malaria kills hundreds of thousands of people each year!

Slime molds are protists that start life as a microscopic, single cell. But sometimes, a single slime mold cell can grow to become a larger blob!

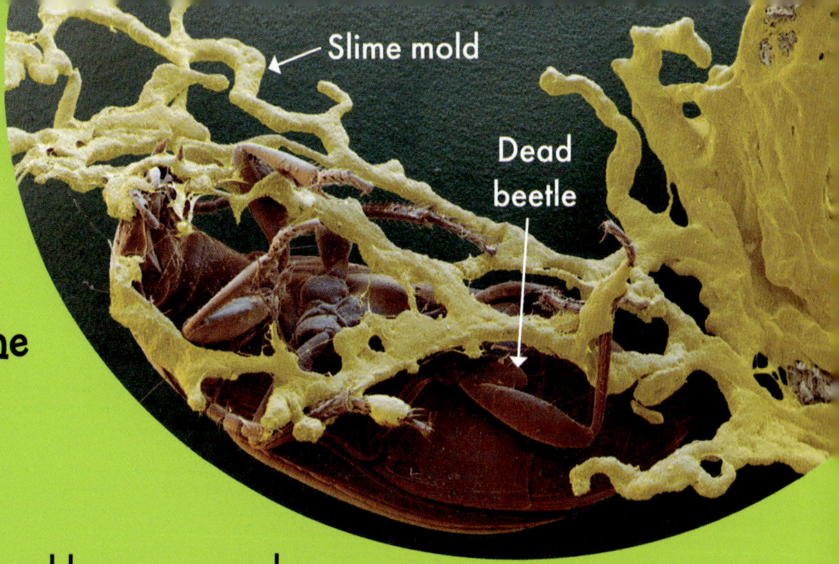

A slime mold oozes over dead leaves, wood, and even animals. It feeds on the fungi and bacteria that live on dead stuff.

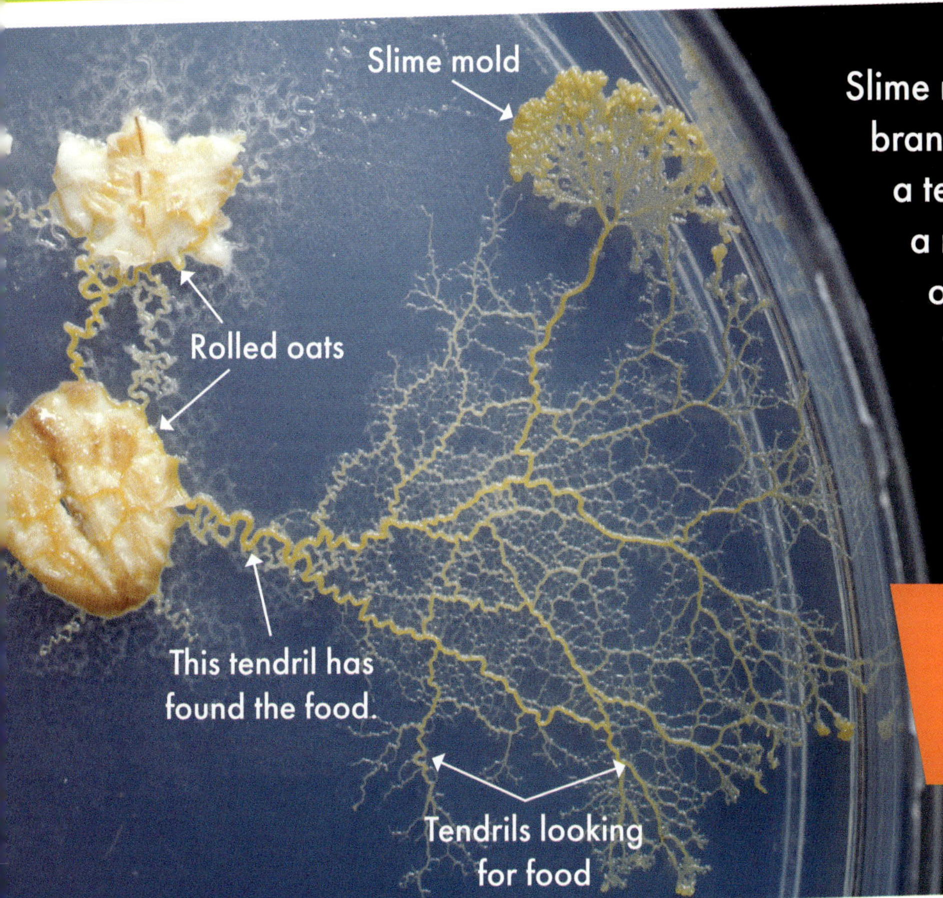

Slime molds send out branch-like tendrils. Once a tendril finds food, it sends a message through the rest of the slime. The other tendrils then ooze to the food—always taking the shortest path.

A slime mold in a petri dish. The tendrils will soak up nutrients from the food.

To test their ability to figure out the quickest route from one place to another, scientists put slime molds into mazes with food. Even though a slime mold doesn't have a brain, it's always able to solve the maze and find the food!

Superhero Fungi

Mushrooms, toadstools, and molds are all fungi. So is yeast that we use for making bread.

You don't need a microscope to see a mushroom. But some fungi are so tiny, they are microbes.

Vegan sausages made from fungi microbes

A microbial fungus is used to make substitutes for meat. The fungus is mixed with other ingredients such as flour or potatoes.

Vegetarians and vegans, who don't eat meat, can cook meals with this meat-substitute.

People with an illness called diabetes may not produce enough of a substance called insulin. Scientists can put human DNA into a yeast cell. The cell then acts like a tiny insulin factory and produces human insulin. Diabetic people inject themselves with this insulin.

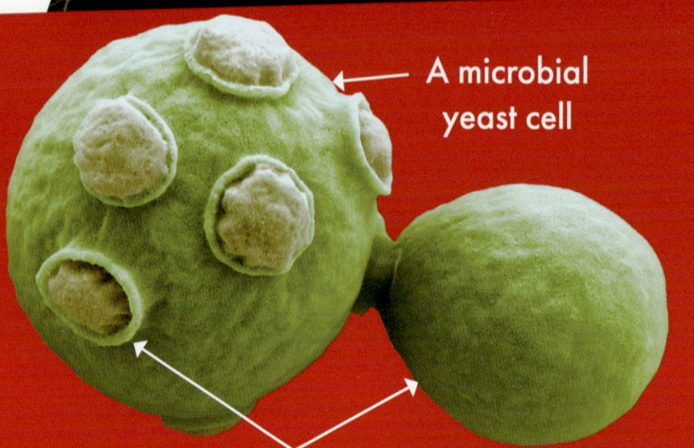

There's one all-time amazing fungus—Penicillium. Scientists estimate that this superhero microbe has saved more than 500 million lives!

Sir Alexander Fleming in 1943

In 1928, a Scottish scientist named Alexander Fleming returned to his laboratory after a vacation. He noticed some mold growing on a petri dish of bacteria. The Penicillium mold was keeping the bacteria from growing. He discovered the mold could even kill bacteria.

All-time Superhero

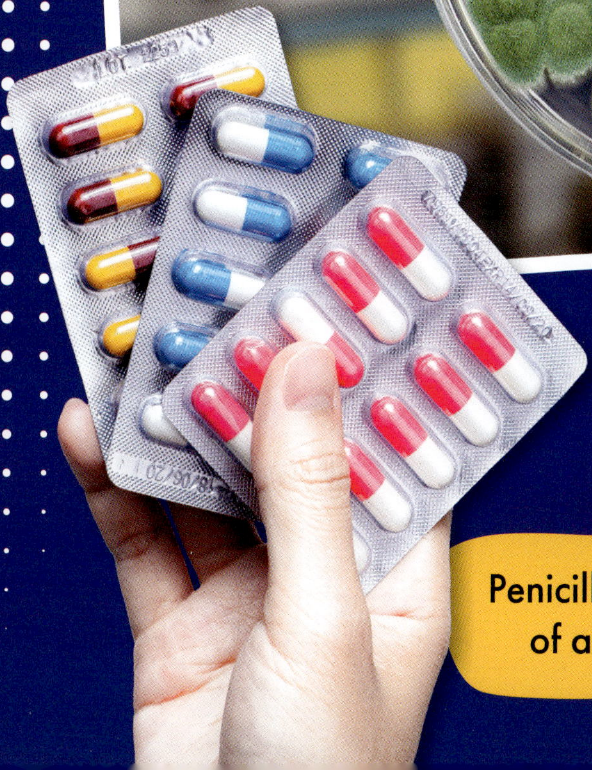

Fleming's accidental discovery was used to develop penicillin. This bacteria-killing wonder drug is used to cure infections.

Penicillin is a type of antibiotic.

You Are a Superhero Universe!

A human body is like a microbial superhero universe. The 38 trillion microbes that live in and on your body are known as your microbiome.

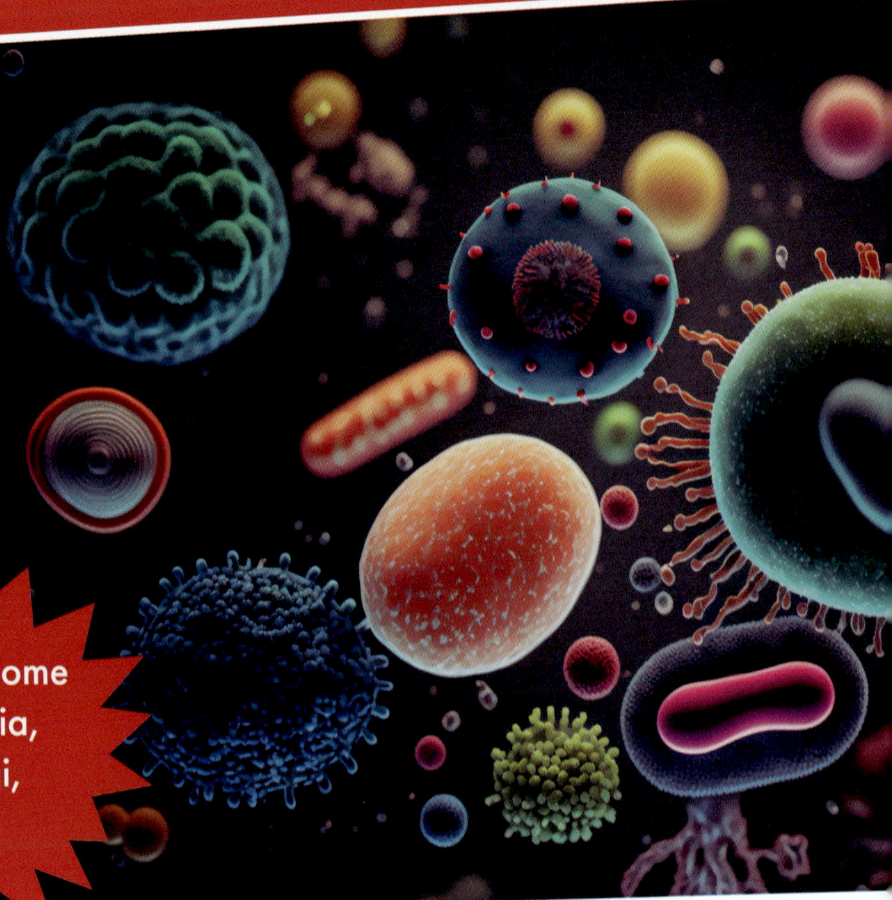

A human microbiome includes bacteria, archaea, fungi, and viruses.

A newborn baby does not have a microbiome. However, as soon as it's born, a baby picks up some microbes from its mother's body. Then gradually the baby's microbiome builds up.

Everyone's microbiome is unique. We take in microbes from our food. We also pick up microbes from our family and friends, our home—even our pets.

Bacteria multiply quickly. In just a few hours, one bacterium can reproduce and become millions!

The microbes in our stomach and digestive system are called our gut microbiome.

The bacteria that live here help us digest our food and take nutrients from it. They also help fight off bacteria that can make us sick.

Eating fruits, vegetables, nuts, grains, and yogurt keeps your gut microbiome happy and your body healthy. It can even improve your mental health.

Meet Your Microbiome

Your body is home to thousands of tiny microbial communities. There are good guys that keep you alive. Bad guys on the attack. And some that are just plain weird or yucky!

They may be tiny, but microbes usually have long, complicated names.

Demodex face mites

These microscopic, eight-legged animals are included in our microbiome. They feed on dead skin cells and grease. They live in the follicles where your hair, eyelashes, and eyebrows grow.

Streptococcus mutans

Feeds on sugars in your mouth and produces lactic acid. This substance can dissolve your tooth enamel.

Staphylococcus aureus

Bacteria that live on our skin. Can be harmless but may also cause skin infections, stomach illnesses, and even serious diseases such as pneumonia and sepsis.

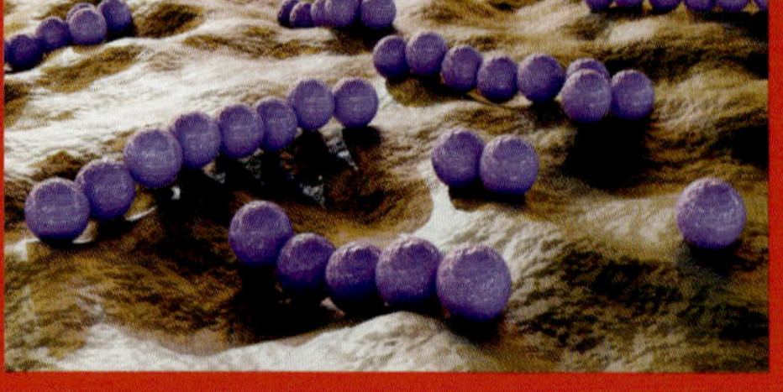

Streptococcal pharyngitis

Causes throat infections.

There are almost as many bacteria in your mouth as there are humans on Earth!

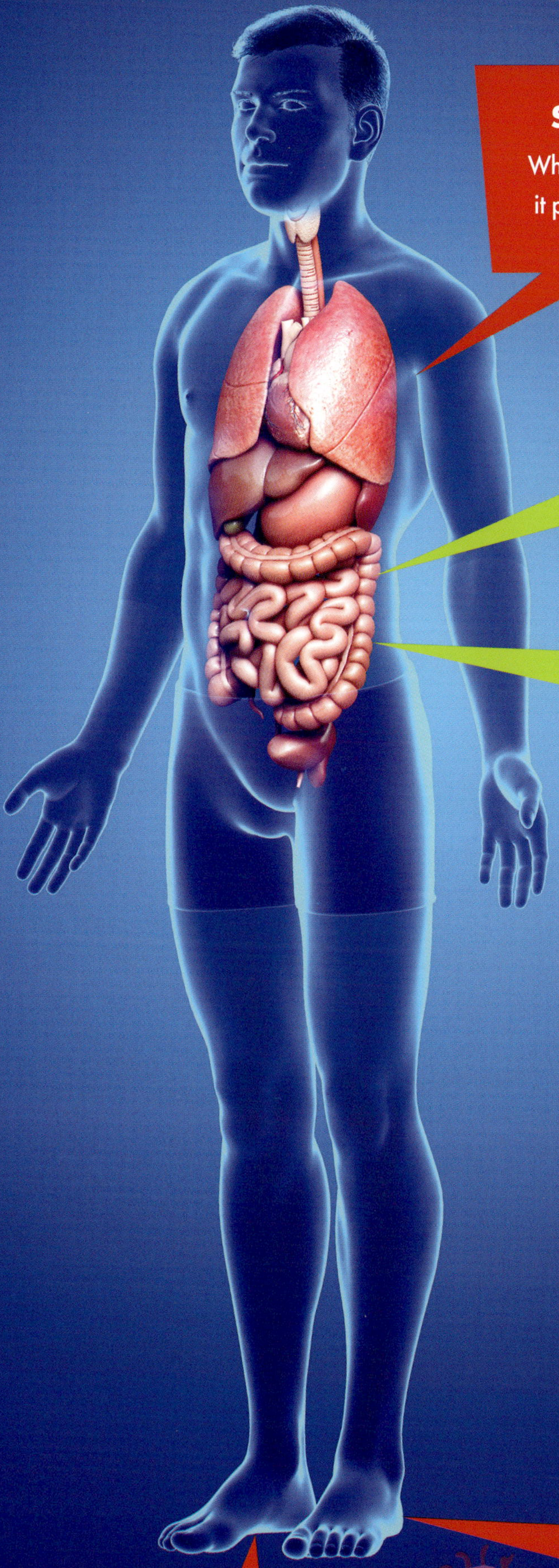

Staphylococcus hominis

When it comes into contact with sweat, it produces yucky smells—body odor!

Lactobacteria

Break down food, absorb nutrients, fight off bad microbes.

Bifidobacteria

Help you digest fiber and poop regularly. Fight bad bacteria. Produce gas that leaves your body as farts!

About one-third of your poop is made up of dead bacteria.

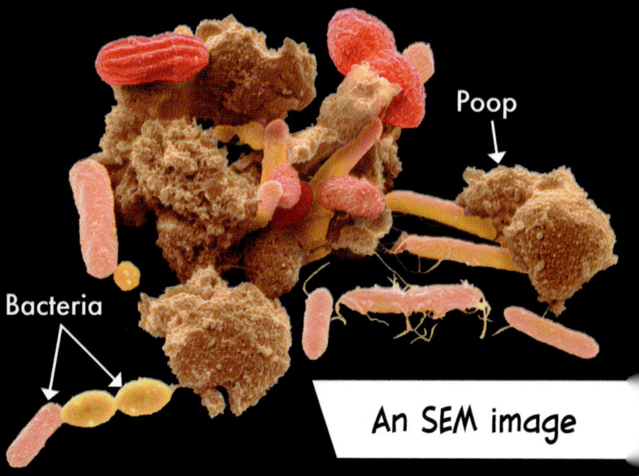

An SEM image

Staphylococcus epidermidis

Breaks down a substance in sweat from feet and makes a cheesy smell.

Tinea pedis

This fungus causes feet to itch and burn, and the skin to crack—especially between the toes. It's nicknamed athlete's foot.

Making Food With Microbes

We can thank microbes for many of the foods we eat!

Yogurt

When Lactobacillus bacteria are added to milk, they produce lactic acid. This substance thickens the milk and turns it into yogurt.

Swiss cheese

Bacteria are also added to milk to turn it into cheese. The bacteria in Swiss cheese produce carbon dioxide gas bubbles that create the holes!

Blue cheese

Remember amazing Penicillium mold? This mold is added to some cheeses during cheese-making. Then the mold grows through the cheese.

The Penicillium microbes make the grayish-blue veins and give the cheese its strong flavor.

Penicillium mold

We even use microbes to make bread.

Yeast is added to bread dough. As the yeast feeds on sugars in the dough, it produces carbon dioxide gas. The gas makes the dough rise.

And without microbes, we wouldn't have chocolate!

Chocolate is made from cocoa beans that grow on trees. The trees grow large pods filled with the beans, or seeds.

Cocoa beans fermenting

When making chocolate, the beans and pulp from the pods are fermented. During fermentation, yeasts and bacteria get to work, breaking down the soft, slimy pulp. This creates heat and special substances.

The fermentation process changes the flavor of the beans from bitter to a delicious chocolate flavor.

Cleaning Up Planet Earth

Superheroes help save the world. So how do microbes do this?

Fighting Climate Change

Microbes called cyanobacteria help fight climate change by taking carbon dioxide gas out of the atmosphere. Just like plants, cyanobacteria use water, carbon dioxide, and sunlight to make food for energy. This process is called photosynthesis.

Cyanobacteria growing in a petri dish

Earth is getting too warm because of harmful gases in its atmosphere. One of these gases is carbon dioxide.

Cyanobacteria also do something else that is amazing. As they photosynthesize, they produce the oxygen we need to breathe.

Fixing Plastic Pollution

Grass and other plants that cows eat contain a natural, plastic-like material called cutin. Microbes that live in the stomachs of cows break down cutin.

Scientists discovered that these microbes can also break down plastic that's used to make items such as soda bottles and plastic bags.

One day, this discovery might help solve the problem of plastic pollution!

Cleaning Up the Ocean

There's one super-big bacterium that's enormous—for a microbe! It's 100 times bigger than an average-sized bacterium, and can be seen without a microscope.

These microbes live in mud off the coast of Namibia, Africa. They feed on hydrogen sulfide gas.

By feeding on this toxic gas, the bacteria help clean up the water for fish and other sealife.

The bacteria form chains.

An illustration of Thiomargarita namibiensis compared to a dime

Superheroes With Superpowers

Wow! I am seriously impressed by microbes. What else can these tiny superheroes do?

G-Force? No Problem!

Astronauts must be able to withstand a force called G-force (g) when they blast into space. Jet pilots feel this force, too.

Pilots and astronauts take a super-fast, spinning ride in a huge centrifuge machine to test their ability to survive high G-forces. These superhero humans can take a force of about 9g. More than this can kill a person!

Scientists tested E. coli bacteria in a small laboratory centrifuge. They discovered these tiny tough guys can survive a G-force of 400,000g!

The Rock Eaters

Microbes have been found in Lake Whillans in Antarctica. They live in total darkness, buried under half a mile (800 m) of solid ice.

You might think there is nothing to feed on in this extreme world. However, scientists discovered that the lake regularly empties and fills up. When this happens, the flowing water wears away and breaks up rocks.

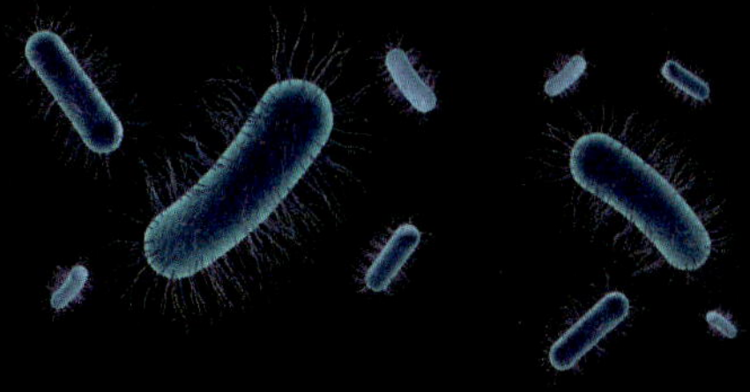

The crushed rocks release chemicals and gases, such as methane and carbon dioxide, that the microbes feed on.

Bacteria Batteries

Geobacter bacteria live underwater in sand and rocks. When these bacteria feed, they make waste. But these tiny microbes don't make poop. The waste material they create is electricity!

Scientists are using these microbes to develop bacteria-powered batteries.

This toy car is being powered by bacteria.

The Ground Beneath Our Feet

There's one very important job that microbes do in our world. They help make the ground beneath our feet!

Soil is made of tiny bits of rock. It also contains rotting organic matter, such as dead leaves. When plants and animals die, microbes help break down this material and make it part of the soil.

There are more microbes in a teaspoon of soil than there are people on Earth.

The work of microbes and small animals, such as worms, turns organic matter into nutrients that feed trees and other plants.

The study of microbes is called microbiology. It's an exciting science because new things are being learned all the time.

A microbiologist collecting a soil sample

Soil microbes reproducing in a petri dish

Microbiologists estimate there could be one trillion different species of microbes on Earth.

1,000,000,000,000

And most of them are still waiting to be discovered.

That is super cool. I want to be a microbiologist and one day discover a new superhero microbe!

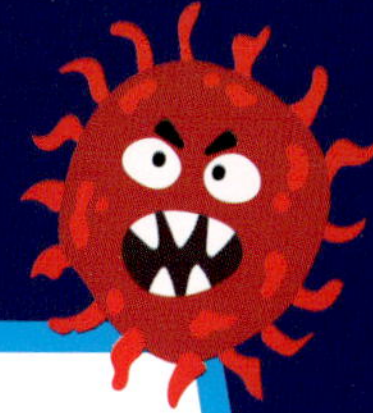

So how do we avoid super-villain microbes getting into our bodies?

Great question! Here are some ways to protect yourself and others.

- Always sneeze or cough into a tissue, and then throw it away.
- Sneezing or coughing into your upper sleeve or the crook of your elbow keeps germs off your hands, too.

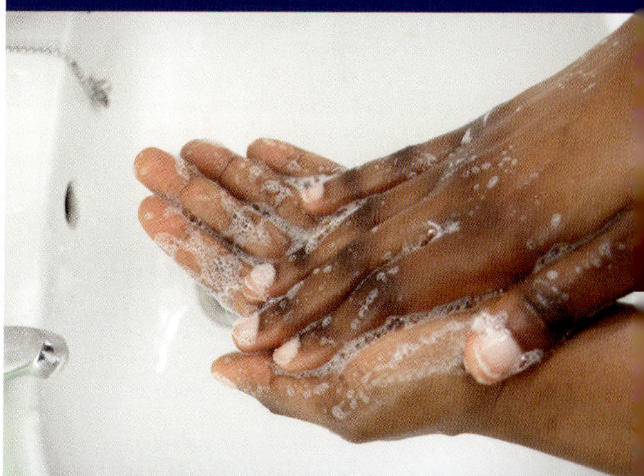

- Wash your hands with soap after going to the bathroom, before making food, before eating, and after touching animals.

Glossary

acidic

Containing substances called acids. Some acids, such as citric acid that gives lemons their sharp, sour taste, are not usually harmful. Other acids can harm living things.

antibiotic

A type of medicine that kills bacteria or keeps them from spreading. Some bacteria cause infections in the human body.

archaeon

A single-celled living thing that is similar to a bacterium. Archaea are found in extreme environments, but some species live in places such as soil or the human body.

bacterium

A microscopic living thing that is made of only one cell. Some bacteria can make us sick, but most are helpful.

carbon dioxide

A colorless gas in the air that is a natural part of Earth's atmosphere.

cell

A tiny part of a living thing. Humans are made of trillions of cells. Microbes may be made of just a single cell.

climate change

A change in Earth's temperature and weather that happens over a long period of time. Climate change can happen naturally, but at the moment, Earth's temperature is getting warmer primarily because of human actions.

cyanobacteria

Bacteria that are able to make food by photosynthesis with water, carbon dioxide gas, and sunlight. As they photosynthesize, they make oxygen.

DNA

A set of instructions inside the cells of living things that tells cells how to look, work, and grow. DNA stands for deoxyribonucleic acid.

fungus

A living thing such as a mushroom, toadstool, mold, or yeast. Some types of fungi are so tiny they are microbes.

G-force (Gravitational force)

The invisible force that pulls things down to the ground.

germ

A type of microbe that can cause a disease and make us sick.

global warming

The gradual increase (over many years) of temperatures on Earth. Climate change is causing global warming.

hydrothermal vent

A crack in the ocean floor that allows super-hot water from inside Earth's crust to spurt out.

microbe

A microscopic living thing such as a bacterium, archaeon, fungus, protist, or virus (although some scientists do not think viruses are alive).

microbiome

The collection of microbes that live in and on your body.

microscopic

Only visible through a microscope.

nutrients

Substances that are needed by living things to help them grow and stay healthy.

organic matter

Rotting material from things that were once alive, such as plants and animals.

oxygen

A colorless gas in the air that is a natural part of Earth's atmosphere. Humans and animals need oxygen to breathe.

pandemic

An infectious disease that affects people worldwide, or over a very large area or number of countries.

parasite

A living thing that lives on or in another life form and feeds on it.

pollution

Trash, liquids, gases, or other substances and materials that are harmful to living things and to the land, water, or air.

protist

A single-celled, microscopic living thing. Protists are not plants, animals, or fungi.

species

A type of living thing. The members of a species look alike and can reproduce together.

virus

A microbe that can only survive inside the cells of living things. Many viruses cause diseases.

Index